KARATE
BASICS

KARATE BASICS

by

Thomas J. Nardi, Ph.D.

Photographs by
David J. Garr

Drawings by
Michael Petronella

Created and Produced by
Arvid Knudsen

Prentice-Hall, Inc.
Englewood Cliffs, New Jersey

Dedication:
This book is lovingly dedicated to my son Tommy

Special thanks to the following people who contributed their time and knowledge to this project: Julissa Betancourt, Tommy DeGaray, Terri Lindquist, Domingo Llanos, Tommy Nardi, Louanne Piantadosi, and Jose Ramirez.

Book design by Arvid Knudsen

Printed in the United States of America   *J

Prentice-Hall International, Inc., London
Prentice-Hall of Australia, Pty. Ltd., Sydney
Prentice-Hall Canada, Inc., Toronto
Prentice-Hall of India Private Ltd., New Delhi
Prentice-Hall of Japan, Inc., Tokyo
Prentice-Hall of Southeast Asia Pte. Ltd., Singapore

Whitehall Books Limited, Wellington, New Zealand
Editora Prentice-Hall Do Brasil LTDA., Rio de Janeiro

10 9 8 7 6 5 4 3 2 1

Library of Congress Cataloging in Publication Data

Nardi, Thomas J.
    Karate basics.

    Summary: Discusses the background and the current styles and modes of this ancient discipline. Also describes the basic techniques, exercises, and the necessary preparation and training.
    1. Karate—Juvenile literature. [1. Karate]
I. Petronella, Mike, ill. II. Title.
GV1114.3.N37   1984   796.8'153   84-6929
ISBN 0-13-514548-1

CONTENTS

INTRODUCTION

Before We Begin

A Word to Parents and Students

As a psychologist, I have found that karate training often provides many benefits to youngsters beyond that offered by other sports. The introverted youngster often begins to blossom when he or she learns karate. The structured drills that involve punching, kicking, and yelling help the youngster overcome shyness and timidity. The anxious or worried child becomes more confident and assertive as he learns to move and control his body. He or she learns to work and compete with others in a friendly and safe environment. Self-confidence and self-esteem grow. Many parents report a marked increase in the child's social interactions. The youngster feels less threatened by other children or new situations. As a result, there is often more of a willingness to become more involved with others.

The extroverted youngster has a safe, healthy outlet in which to compete with himself and others. Youngsters are taught how to avoid trouble and challenges. They learn to have enough self-confidence that they need not respond to teasing or provocation from peers.

The aggressive child is taught the self-discipline that aids in keeping anger under control. He or she learns that fighting is merely a way of showing off and that showing off is a sign of low self-esteem and a lack of self-confidence.

Karate training is a gross motor activity that helps youngsters develop a sense of integrity about their bodies. Balance, coordination, posture, and general movements improve with karate training. The pre-adolescent, in particular, finds that karate training helps him or her cope with the clumsiness that often accompanies the spurt of growth at this age.

Karate also offers an additional bonus that other sports do not provide. Karate teaches self-defense. In the unsettling times in which we live, a knowledge of how to protect oneself can be crucial. Parents often report feeling more secure knowing their sons or daughters are capable of defending themselves.

Encourage and support your youngster's involvement. You will be pleasantly surprised with the results. And, who knows, you may want to try a class yourself!

Thomas J. Nardi

1 A Brief History of Karate

No one really knows how karate began. One legend states that an Indian monk named Ta Mo traveled to China in 525 A.D. to introduce the concepts of Zen Buddhism. Towards this goal, Ta Mo established the Shaolin Monastery in the Honan Province of China.

Ta Mo discovered that many of the Chinese were too frail or sickly to accept the demands of monastic life. He was also concerned about the large numbers of marauding bandits who plagued the area around the temple. Ta Mo and the monks believed in nonviolence. Their religion forbade them to carry or use weapons. Thus, the monks were easy prey for the bandits. Ta Mo decided to do something about this situation.

Ta Mo noted that wild animals were always in top physical condition. "What was their secret?" he wondered. He observed animals such as the tiger, crane, and snake. He then realized that they did indeed have a secret. Animals perform certain movements that involve the stretching and tensing of their muscles. Ta Mo devised a series of exercises that imitated the movements of various animals. The exercises also copied the way these animals protected themselves. The monks soon discovered that they could use the same movements to protect themselves. Ta Mo's exercises made the monks healthier and stronger, while at the same time providing them with a means of self-defense without the use of weapons.

Various forms of the exercises taught at the Shaolin Temple spread throughout China. The exercises were practiced both as a way of improving one's health and as a method of self-defense. Today, in the United States these systems are referred to as *kung fu.*

While these styles were developing in China, other Asian countries were practicing their own native systems of self-defense. On the island of Okinawa the people practiced a fighting system called *Te*. "Te" means "hands," implying that the hand was the principal weapon used.

Japan, meanwhile, also had a weaponless system of self-defense called *ju-jitsu*. It taught how to use the attacker's own strength to defeat him. Ju-jitsu involved the use of throws, punches, kicks, and joint locking techniques.

In 1882, a Japanese college professor named Jigoro Kano decided to transform ju-jitsu from a system of self-defense to a sport. Kano removed the dangerous punching and kicking movements from ju-jitsu. He then modified the grappling and throwing techniques to create the sport of judo. In 1964 it became a recognized Olympic sport.

In the early 1920s the Japanese had become very curious about the Okinawan systems of Te. They invited many of the Te experts to visit Japan to demonstrate their art. The Okinawans began to refer to their art as "karate" when they exported it to Japan. The word "karate" consists of two Japanese words, "kara," meaning "empty," and "te" meaning "hands." Hence the term karate was used to signify the art of empty-hand fighting. It is an empty-hand system in that no weapons are used, other than the natural "weapons" of the body: the hands, knees, feet, etc.

The Japanese became very impressed by the effectiveness of karate. Many styles and variations of Okinawan karate were developed in Japan.

The Koreans were also influenced by contact with neighboring China's kung fu. The Koreans developed *tae kwon do*, which means "the art of kicking and punching."

A more recent off-shoot of karate is called kick-boxing. Kick-boxing combines the kicks of karate with the punches of boxing. They make full contact with their punches and kicks in an attempt to score points or knock out their opponents. Kick-boxing should not be confused with true karate.

It is inaccurate to say that one type of karate is better than another. *Kung fu, karate,* and *tae kwon do* are all exciting sports and effective systems of self-defense. There are certain similarities and differences among all three. One thing in common to all, however, is an emphasis on respecting others, avoiding trouble, and maintaining self-control.

Goju-Ryu Karate

Chojun Miyagi was born in the Okinawan city of Naha on April 25, 1888. He devoted himself to studying *Naha Te*, the fighting system of his city. Even after mastering Naha Te, Miyagi wanted to learn more. In

CHOJUN MIYAGI,
FOUNDER OF
GOJU KARATE

order to further his knowledge he went to China in 1915. He studied various forms of kung fu for two years before returning to his homeland.

Soon, Miyagi began teaching a form of karate that combined kung fu and Naha Te. He called his style of karate *goju-ryu*. In Japanese, "go" means "hard" or "strong," and "ju" means "soft" or "gentle." The word "ryu" means "style." Thus Miyagi taught the hard-soft style of karate. The term "goju" comes from a line in an ancient Chinese poem: "Everything in the universe is breathing hard and soft."

Miyagi was a great master of karate, but he also understood philosophy and psychology. He believed that to be happy or successful in life, a person had to know when to be "hard" and when to be "soft." That is, a person had to know when to stand up against others and when to give in; when to talk and when to listen; when to act and when to wait. Miyagi believed that it was important to know when to fight but it was more important to know when not to fight.

Miyagi first introduced goju-ryu karate to Japan in 1928. In 1934, he introduced it to Hawaii. Other people mastered goju-ryu and introduced it to different parts of the mainland United States in the late 1950s and early 1960s. Today goju-ryu karate schools can be found in countries all over the world. Each school, called a "dojo" in Japanese, will have a picture of Master Miyagi on display. Each class will begin and end with a bow to the picture of Miyagi. This bow is to show respect to the memory of the founder of goju-ryu who died on October 8, 1953.

The remainder of this book will teach the basics of goju-ryu karate as it is practiced in hundreds of dojo around the world.

11

2 Traditions and Etiquette

There are many traditions associated with the practice of karate. Some of these traditions may seem strange to the new student. It is helpful to remember that the traditions are very, very old. They are designed to remind the student of karate's heritage of character building and discipline.

Following the traditions shows respect for the original roots of karate. It is also a way of ensuring that the student learns in a responsible and enjoyable manner.

Meditation

Most karate classes began and end with a brief period of meditation. During meditation the students sit quietly with their eyes closed. Sitting quietly without moving teaches patience and self-control. Meditation also teaches the student how to relax. During meditation the student has a chance to "clear his mind." That is, to put aside other thoughts and prepare himself to learn karate. Karate training requires concentration and attention. The student will not want to be distracted during his or her training by any other thoughts. By sitting quietly, relaxing, and putting aside other thoughts, the student will be better able to pay full attention to what will be taught in class.

At the end of the class students again meditate. This meditation period gives them a chance to relax their bodies and minds.

Kiai: The Karate Shout

Did you ever notice what happens when you have to lift something heavy? You probably grunted, sighed, or exhaled loudly as you exerted yourself. Karate masters long ago noticed the same phenomenon. The karate masters investigated it and discovered some interesting things. They found that forcefully exhaling could help focus energy and strength. They also found that a short, sharp yell could enhance the exhalation. Hence they discovered the *kiai*, or the karate shout. It is a way of showing determination, concentration, and effort.

Karate teachers will often have their students kiai when performing certain punching or kicking techniques. The kiai tightens the stomach muscles and gives more power to the techniques. In a self-defense situation the kiai can bring others to your assistance. It can also help in frightening away an attacker.

The kiai is made by exhaling forcefully as you shout a particular sound or word. The sounds "huh" and "uts" are often used in doing the kiai.

The Bow

Karate classes always begin and end with a bow. The students begin class with the bow to their instructor, to a picture of the founder of their style of karate, and to the flag of their country. The students will bow to each other before and after they practice together. The bow is more than the Oriental equivalent of shaking hands. It is the traditional way of expressing respect and courtesy to others. The bow can be made from either a standing or a sitting position.

The Karate Oath

Another tradition is the recitation of the karate oath, called the "dojo kun." Many karate classes will either begin or end with all the students repeating the dojo kun. The students are encouraged to memorize the dojo kun and apply it to their daily lives.

The goju-ryu dojo kun is as follows:
1. We are proud to study the way of the hard and soft.
2. We shall always show courtesy to all.
3. We shall be quick to take advantage of opportunity.
4. We shall always practice patience.
5. We shall always respect the spirit of karate.

13

The Uniform

The karate uniform is called a *gi* (pronounced "gee"). The gi is made of fairly strong material. It is designed in such a way that it will not rip when you stretch, jump, or kick. The gi is based upon the traditional everyday clothing worn in Okinawa and Japan. The traditional color of the gi is white, although some styles of karate use a black gi.

The Belt System

Karate employs different color belts to indicate different levels of ability and achievement. Beginners start with a white belt. As they progress, they will be tested for promotion to a higher rank. If they can demonstrate that they have learned the basics, and if they have developed the proper attitude, their instructor will award them the next higher belt. In goju-ryu karate, children progress from a white belt through yellow, orange, green, blue, purple, brown, and finally, a black belt.

The black belt signifies an expert with many years of experience. However, there are many levels of black belt. The lowest level is the first-degree black belt; the highest level is the tenth degree. The tenth degree is reserved for the true master who has devoted his entire life to karate. Usually only the founder of a particular system is awarded a tenth degree. Master Miyagi, the founder of goju-ryu karate, was acknowledged by other karate experts to be a tenth degree.

The various levels of black belt serve to remind the practitioners that there is no end to the learning process. Even when they achieve a black belt, they know there is always more to learn. Black belts strive to master new techniques while they continue to perfect what they have already been taught.

Counting

When doing certain exercises or drills, many karate teachers will call out the count in Japanese. Here are the numbers from one to ten in Japanese and with the pronunciation indicated in parentheses.

1. ichi (*ee-chee*)
2. ni (*nee*)
3. san (*sahn*)
4. shi (*shee*)
5. go (*goh*)

6. roku (*roh-koo*)
7. shichi (*shee-chee*)
8. hachi (*hah-chee*)
9. ku (*koo*)
10. ju (*joo*)

3 Karate Exercises

Warm-up Exercises

Following the meditation period, karate students perform a series of warm-up exercises. The warm-ups loosen the various joints of the body while stretching the muscles. Five or ten minutes of warm-ups ensure that the body will be ready for the vigorous punching and kicking movements that are to follow. At the end of class the same exercises are repeated to help the body cool down after the workout.

Each of the following exercises should be repeated at least ten times each. Do the movements slowly. Do not use jerky, bouncing movements. Remember, you are only trying to warm up and prepare your body for further work.

Neck Exercise: Side

Stand with your feet spread and your hands on your belt. Slowly neck stretch. Gradually try to bring your ear to your shoulder. You won't lean your head to one side. You will feel the muscles in the side of your be able to do this, but it will provide a gentle stretch to your neck. Repeat the movement on the other side. Alternate from one side to the other. Go slowly!

Neck Exercise: Forward and Back

Stand as before and slowly tip the neck backward and then forward so that the chin touches the chest. Repeat ten times.

Neck Rotation

Stand with your feet apart and your hands on your belt. Bring your chin to your chest, then rotate the head to the right, then backwards, then to the left. Circle the head slowly in both a clockwise and counterclockwise position. This exercise helps rid the neck of any stiffness.

Chest Exercise

Stand with feet apart, and with the right arm above the left in front of the chest. Swing both elbows back at the same time. This will stretch and strengthen the muscles of the chest. Return the arms to their position

in front of the chest, but this time put the left arm on top. Swing both elbows back again. Each time you return the arms to their position in front of the chest, alternate the left and right arm on top. This alternating helps develop coordination. Repeat these for ten counts.

Hip and Waist Exercise: Rotations

Place both hands on your hips and then rotate your hips in a circle to the left and then to the right. Repeat ten times. This helps maintain flexibility in the waist. It also helps trim the waistline.

Hip and Waist Exercise: Bending

Next, keep both hands on the hips and bend slowly backward. Lean as far backward as is comfortable. Stay in the back-bending position for

the count of two. Then bend forward and grab your ankles. Try to bring your head to your knees. Hold this position for a count of six before returning to an upright position. Repeat this exercise ten times.

Trunk Rotations

Stand with the feet apart, about twice the width of your shoulders. Grasp your arms overhead. Lean to your right, then make a big circular motion as you bend forward, then come up on your left to the starting position. Alternate circling to the right and left until you have made a total of ten circles. This will also help trim your waistline.

Leg Exercises: Squats

Stand with the feet apart, about twice the width of your shoulders and with the hands extended out in front of the body. Squat straight downward, then return to start position. Repeat ten times. This exercise will increase the strength in your legs.

Single-Leg Stretch

Stand with the feet far apart. Then lean onto the right knee, stretching the left leg. This stretches the inner thigh muscle and will help make kicking easier. Keep the left foot flat on the ground. Then shift to the other side. That is, lean onto the left knee and stretch the right leg. Repeat five times on each side.

Lean onto the right knee again and this time point the toes of the left foot straight up. This will give the thigh a different type of stretch. Then repeat on the opposite side. Alternate five times on each side.

Split

Start with your feet as far apart as is comfortable. Slowly try to lower yourself even further. Be careful to move very slowly! Keep both feet flat on the floor at first. Later you can point the toes upward to put a different emphasis on the muscles being stretched. Never try to force yourself to go lower than is comfortable for you. Progress takes time. With persistent practice you may eventually be able to do a full split.

Strengthening Exercise: Upper Body

You do not need to lift weights or do a lot of different exercises in order to increase your strength. The simple push-up is a standard exercise

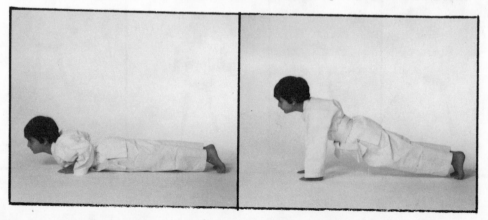

in all karate classes. The push-up strengthens the entire upper body: chest, shoulders, arms, and back muscles.

Start with your palms flat on the floor below your chest. Then straighten your arms to lift your chest off the floor. Keep your back straight. Lower and raise your chest by bending and straightening your arms. Start with as many as you can do and gradually build up to twenty or twenty-five repetitions.

Strengthening Exercise: Abdomen

Sit-ups strengthen and trim the midsection of the body. Firm abdominal muscles will help to protect you from accidental blows to the midsection.

One way of doing sit-ups is to have someone hold your feet while you lie on your back. It is important to keep the knees bent when you do sit-ups. If sit-ups are done with the legs straight, you may hurt your lower back. Place your hands behind your head and keep your back off the floor. Then curl your upper body forward to a full sitting position before returning to the start position.

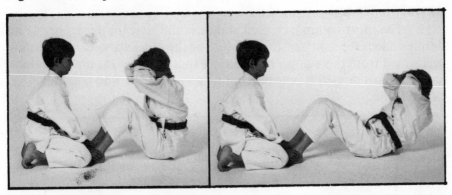

In karate, sit-ups are often done with a partner. Two students will wrap their feet around each other's legs while in a sitting position. They then will lean backwards. They will keep tension on their abdominal muscles by not letting their upper backs touch the floor. Next, each curls his or her trunk up to the sitting position. It is important that they both come up at the same time, otherwise the exercise is much more difficult to do. This is an excellent way to strengthen the midsection while learning to coordinate your movements with those of another person.

Begin by doing as many sit-ups as possible and gradually build up to doing twenty or twenty-five at a time.

4 Stances

Karate places an important emphasis on maintaining good posture and balance. There are several stances used in karate that give maximum stability, yet also allow for easy maneuverability. The photos show the foot positions of the common stances and the proper body positions for the stances.

Sanchin Dachi

The most commonly used stance is the *sanchin dachi*, or, as it is simply called, the sanchin stance. Most of the blocks and hand strikes are performed from this stance. It is a stance that provides maximum stability. Sanchin is often used when confronting an opponent who is standing very close to you.

In the sanchin stance, the toes of the rear foot point straight ahead, while the toes of the front foot point across the body at a 45-degree angle. When the right foot is forward, it is called a right sanchin stance; when the left foot is forward, it is called a left sanchin stance. The heel of the front foot should be directly across from the toes of the rear foot. The feet should be slightly less than a shoulder's width apart. Your weight should be distributed evenly on both feet.

Try to grip the floor with your toes. Keep your back straight as you tense your hips, thighs, and buttocks. The knees are slightly bowed in to protect the groin area.

Musubi-dachi

The *musubi-dachi* is the attention stance. Stand with your heels together and your feet pointing outward at 45-degree angles. This is the

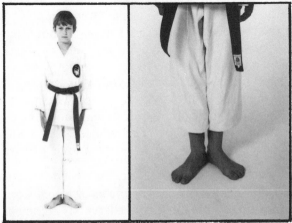

stance used when receiving directions from an instructor. It is also used when bowing to another person.

Shiko-dachi

The *shiko-dachi* is a very wide stance. The feet are apart about twice the width of the shoulders. Point your toes outward at 45-degree angles and lower your hips into a semi-squat. Your weight should be distributed equally on both feet. The shiko-dachi stance resembles the position a person would assume if he were riding on a horse. For this reason it is sometimes referred to as the "horse stance."

The shiko-dachi is used for some striking and blocking techniques. The stance can be uncomfortable at first. However, if you continue to practice it, you will be surprised at how strong your legs will become.

Zenkutsu-dachi

The *zenkutsu-dachi* is the forward stance. It is frequently referred to simply as the zenkutsu stance. The forward foot is about two foot-lengths from the rear foot. The feet are about a shoulder-width apart. If the left foot is forward, it is called a left zenkutsu; if the right foot is forward, it is called a right zenkutsu. In zenkutsu you lean forward, bending the front leg and bracing yourself with your rear leg. The front leg should be bent so that the knee is directly over the toes. Remember to keep your back straight. About 70 percent of your weight should be on the front foot and 30 percent on the rear foot. This stance gives a lot of power and stability to punches and kicks when you are moving forward.

Neko Ashi Dachi

The words "neko ashi dachi" means the "cat foot stance." The feet are thought to resemble those of a cat who is getting ready to pounce on its prey. The rear foot is flat on the floor and the front heel is off the ground. The feet are fairly close together, with 95 percent of the body's weight on the rear foot and only 5 percent on the ball of the front foot. Keep your back straight as you crouch down in this stance.

This stance is often used in sparring practice because it allows for quick movements forward, backwards, and to the sides.

5 Blocking Techniques

Karate is the art of self-defense. Therefore, it puts a major emphasis on defensive techniques. Being able to block or ward off an attacker's blows is of prime importance.

Practice the blocks slowly until the movements become comfortable for you. It is important to coordinate the movement of the left and right hands, so that the blocks are completed as the opposite hand is withdrawn to the chest.

High Block

The high block is used to protect yourself from blows to the face and head area. Start with your right foot forward in a sanchin stance. Bend your right arm and hold it palm up towards the right side of your body. Your left hand should be placed near your chest. Bring your left hand to

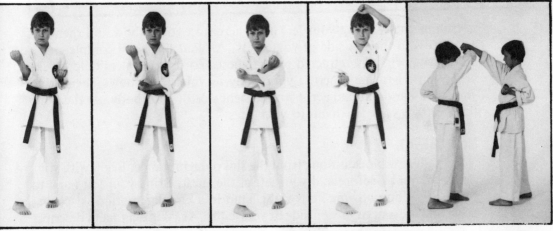

your right elbow. Then bring your left arm upward in a circular motion across and to the left of your facial area. As your left hand moves to do the block, your right hand is retracted to your chest. Stop your left hand above your head. Your left fist should be about one fist's width from the top of your forehead.

Next bring the right hand across to below your left elbow. Then move it upward in a circular motion to the right side of your head. At the same time the left hand is retracted to the chest. Again, the fist of the blocking arm is about a fist's width from the top of your forehead.

Middle Block

The middle block is used to protect the chest and stomach area from an opponent's strike. Start as before in a right sanchin stance with your right arm palm up towards the side of your body and your left fist

near your chest. Bring your left hand across to your elbow and then out and across to the left side of your body. As your left hand completes the block, your right is retracted to the chest. To do a right middle block, bring your right hand across your body to your left elbow. Then bring your right hand out and across to the right side of your body. At the same time, retract your left hand to your chest.

Low Block

The low block is done from the shiko-dachi stance. Begin with your right arm out as before and your left at the chest. Bring your left hand to your right elbow. Swing your right hand in a circular motion, sweeping down and in front of the left side of your body. As your right hand describes

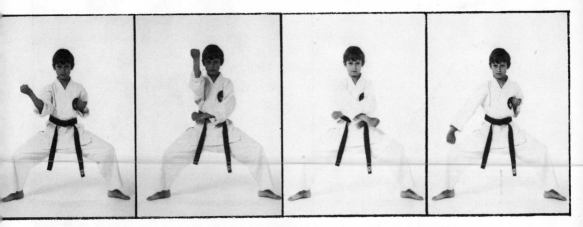

a large circle, your left is pulled to the chest. Your right hand stops over your right knee.

Next bring your right hand to your left elbow and move your left up, across, and downward. It sweeps in front of you in a circular motion, stopping above your left knee. At the same time, your right is retracted to your chest.

This block is used against attacks to the middle and lower portions of the body.

Middle-Low Block Combination

The middle-low block combination is used to improve coordination. It involves a simultaneous middle block with one hand and a low block with the other hand. Start from a right sanchin stance with one arm in the middle-block position and the other in a low-block position. As the lower block comes up on the inside the middle block descends on the outside.

6 Striking Techniques

In karate, striking techniques refer to all blows delivered with the hands. Strikes include punching with the fists as well as chopping with the sides of the hand.

The most widely used karate strike is the basic punch done with the fist. The karate punch is different from the punch commonly used in boxing. In boxing, the entire front surface of the fist is used to land a blow. Karate experts believe that this spreads out the force of the punch, thus reducing its power. In karate the force of the blow is concentrated on the first two big knuckles of the fist. Such a concentration of force allows even a small person to deliver a powerful punch.

There is another difference between the punches used in boxing and those of karate. A boxer will throw his shoulder into a punch. That is, he will twist or lean his body forward to add power to the blow. In karate, the punch is thrown with no shoulder movement. Karate teaches that it is important to maintain a straight-back posture to avoid throwing oneself off balance. Proper balance gives additional power to the karate punch.

Basic Punching Drill

Start by standing in a left sanchin stance. Extend your left arm out in front of you. Keep your right fist beside your chest. Clench both fists. Move your right fist forward, along the side of your ribs keeping the palm side up. At the same time, start to turn your extended left arm over and

begin to retract it to your chest. As your right elbow passes your rib cage, begin to turn your fist so that the palm faces the floor. At the same time, continue to retract your left hand. Stop the movement of your right arm just before it is fully extended. Coordinate the movement between the two hands so that as one goes out, the other returns. Alternate a slow-punching sequence between the two hands.

The basic punch can be directed to the face, solar plexus, or lower abdomen. Use your own body as a guide as to how high or low to punch.

The basic punch can also be done using the shiko-dachi or zenkutsu stances. The punching movements are exactly the same, regardless of which stance you use.

Undercut Strike

There is a variation on the basic punch called the undercut. The undercut is performed from the shiko-dachi stance. The only difference

between the undercut and the basic punch is the position of the striking hand. The undercut is delivered to the lower abdomen, with the striking fist facing palm upwards at the moment of contact.

27

Back-Fist Strikes

Karate has several striking techniques that utilize the back of the fist. Back-fist strikes are usually delivered with a snapping, whip-like motion. It is important to keep the arm and fist relaxed until the moment of contact. At the instant of contact the fist should be clenched tightly. Immediately after contact, relax the fist as it is returned to the starting position.

The first back-fist is to the opponent's facial area. Start by standing in a left sanchin stance with both of your arms close together, the palms facing your chin and chest. Snap your right fist straight forward. Return it to the starting position and then snap your left fist forward. If your fist goes out at ten miles per hour, try to snap it back at fifteen miles per hour.

The second variation on the back-fist strike also begins with the sanchin stance. Stand with your arms bent at the elbow and your fists directly over your shoulders. Look to your right and snap your right fist downward and to the side. Return your hand to the start position and look to the front. Then, look to the left as you snap your left fist downward to the side. This back-fist technique is used to strike at an opponent attacking from the side. The target area would be the face.

The third variation on the back fist is also a strike to the side. This time begin in left sanchin stance with the right fist on top of the left. Hold both fists against the abdomen. Look to the right as you snap your right fist to the side. After the strike, look to the front as you return your right fist to your abdomen, but place it below the left fist. Then, look to the left as you snap your left fist outward. Look to the front as you return your fist to the abdomen. Place your left fist below your right in preparation for another strike to the right. The striking fist is always on top; the return-

ing fist is placed on the bottom. This strike is directed to an opponent's midsection. Use your own solar plexus as a target guide for the strike.

Edge-of-the-Hand Strike

The edge-of-the-hand strike is often called the "karate chop." The traditional karate name for this technique is the *shuto-uchi*. The edge of the hand between the wrist and the point below the little finger is used as the contact area for the strike. Do not make contact with the side of your fingers or you may injure your hand.

Start from a left sanchin stance with your right hand behind your ear and your left hand in front of your body. Swing your right hand around and to the front. At the same time, draw your left hand in to your chest. Stop your right hand directly in front of your neck. Then, bring your left hand up to a point behind your left ear. Swing the left hand around and to the front as you withdraw your right hand to the chest.

This strike could be delivered to an attacker's temple area or the side of his neck.

7   Kicking Techniques

    Karate was designed to provide a small, weak person with a means of defense against larger, stronger opponents. Karate, therefore, utilizes techniques that can provide the smaller person with as many advantages as possible. Karate experts of the past realized that the legs are much stronger and longer than the arms. The legs will give more power and a greater reach against an opponent than will the hands. For these reasons it was only logical that karate would develop several techniques of kicking.

    Kicking is often associated with "dirty fighting." However, it is important to remember that karate techniques, including the kicks, are to be used only when you must defend yourself from danger. Karate should never be used to bully others. The person trained in karate should never be the one to start a fight. Kicking is justified if you have no other way to protect yourself from being seriously injured by an attacker.

Front Kick

    The front kick is the most basic of all kicks. It uses the ball of the foot as the contact area. The kick can be delivered to an opponent's mid-section. The toes are curled back to prevent them from being smashed by contact with the target.

31

Start the front kick by first bringing your hands up in an on-guard position. That is, one hand is extended outward and one is held closer to your body. Your feet should be apart about the width of your shoulders. Lift your right knee straight upward. Then, snap your foot forward. Aim for an area directly in front of the knot of your belt. Do not allow your foot to drop to the floor after you kick. Bring your foot back to where it was, with your knee lifted. Then place your foot on the floor. Lift the other knee, kick, and then bring your foot back to the raised knee position before placing it on the floor. As you kick, change your hand position so that the right hand is forward when you kick with your right foot and the left hand is forward when you kick with your left foot.

Low Side-Kick

The low side-kick is a very good kick for self-defense purposes. It is directed to an attacker's knees or shins. Start with your feet about shoulder-width apart and your hands in an on-guard position with your right hand

forward. Bring your right foot up and place it alongside your left knee. Pivot slightly on your left foot so that your right side turns 45 degrees to the front. Now thrust your right foot downward. The striking area is the edge of your foot.

After you kick, return your right foot to the side of your left knee. Do not drop your foot to the floor after the kick. Return the foot to the position by your knee before lowering the foot to the floor.

Switch your hand positions so that your left hand is slightly forward. Bring your left foot to the right knee, pivot 45 degrees and kick downward. Return your foot to the position beside your knee before placing it on the floor.

High Side-Kick

The high side-kick is performed very much like the low side-kick. One difference between the two lies in the target area. While the low side-kick is directed to the opponent's knee or shin, the high side-kick is directed

to the opponent's rib cage area. Another difference is that the low side-kick is done with a 45-degree pivot of the body to the front. The high side-kick is thrown directly to the side.

Begin by assuming an on-guard stance with the feet shoulder-width apart. Lift the right foot to the height of the left knee. Thrust the right foot directly outward to the side. The height of the kick should be about that of your own rib cage. Return the foot to a position beside your left knee before placing the foot on the floor. The striking area is the side of the foot. Next, lift the left foot to the height of the right knee and then thrust the kick outward. Return to the knee position before placing the foot on the floor.

Round Kick

The round kick is used frequently in sparring practice. Begin by assuming the on-guard position, as before. Lift the right leg so that the thigh is parallel to the floor. Then, pivot your left foot 45 degrees to the left and kick to the front. The ball of the foot takes a circular path to the

target area. Use your belt line as a guide to the proper height for the kick. Bring the foot back so that the thigh is again parallel to the floor. Place your foot on the floor and prepare to kick with the other leg. Lift the left leg so that the thigh is parallel to the floor, kick with a circular motion, return to the thigh-parallel position, then place the foot on the floor.

Balance

It is very important to maintain proper balance when kicking. Avoid leaning too far forward or backward when you kick. Do not let your arms flap about as you kick. If you find yourself losing your balance, try kicking a little lower. Do the kicks slowly, striving for proper form. With consistent practice of the proper form, you will be able to do these kicks with balance, power, and speed.

8 Sparring Techniques

A karate proverb states that "one technique mastered is more valuable than one hundred techniques sampled." Karate emphasizes quality in the performance of a technique over quantity of techniques known. It is much better to be able to do one technique very well than to have a general sense of how to do many different techniques.

Sparring refers to the exchange of defensive and offensive techniques between two students. Sparring practice can include repetition of a basic technique. For example, one student will throw a front kick and the other will block and counterattack. Both students know what the other will do. They work cooperatively to learn the proper form of the technique.

Another way to practice sparring techniques is to allow each student to attack or defend with any technique he or she wishes to use. Neither student knows what the other will do. This is more advanced and should only be done with an instructor present.

The techniques presented in this chapter are basic prerequisites to the development of proficiency in sparring. Read the description of each technique and refer to the pictures for a clearer understanding. Make sure that you and your partner understand what the other will be doing. Practice each technique in slow motion until you both feel comfortable with it. Then, and only then, can you gradually increase the speed with which you do the techniques. Proper form is much more important than speed.

Each session of practicing sparring techniques should begin and end with a bow of respect and courtesy to your partner. Remember, too, that you and your partner are trying to help each other to learn the techniques. Do not try to trick each other when practicing. Be careful that you do not actually hit each other. Stop your strikes and kicks several inches away from your target. Use the kiai shout when you perform your techniques. Take turns practicing the attacker's and defender's roles. Try to develop a slow rhythm to the movements.

Technique #1

Stand facing each other in a left zenkutsu stance. The person on the right throws a basic punch with his right hand. The person on the left

turns slightly and does a high block with her left hand. She then counters with a right punch to the body.

Technique #2

Face each other in a left zenkutsu stance. The person on the left does a front kick with his left leg. The person on the right steps back with her left leg to avoid the kick. At the same time she sweeps the kick aside with her right hand. She then counters with a left punch to the body.

Technique #3

Face each other in a left zenkutsu stance. The person on the right punches with his right hand to get his opponent to react. As she begins to

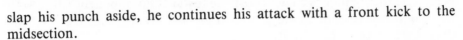

slap his punch aside, he continues his attack with a front kick to the midsection.

Technique #4

Begin by facing each other in a right zenkutsu stance. The person on the left steps forward into another zenkutsu stance with her left leg forward while she punches with her left hand. Her opponent steps back with his right leg and assumes a zenkutsu stance with his left leg forward. He then slaps her left punch away. She then throws a right punch to his body. He counters that punch with a left low block. She then does another punch to his face with her left hand.

Technique #5

Again start by facing each other in a right zenkutsu stance. The person on the right does a backfist strike towards his opponent's face with his right hand. As soon as the opponent lifts her arm to block his strike, he does a side kick to her rib area.

Technique #6

Begin by facing each other in a left zenkutsu stance. The person on the right steps forward with her right foot while punching with her right hand. The person on the left steps back with his left foot and does a middle block. He then grabs her punching arm and counters with a round kick to her midsection.

9 Tournament Competition

After you have been studying karate for awhile you may think about entering tournament competition. Some tournaments are small and have only local schools entering them. Others are quite large with competitors from all over the country attending.

Tournaments provide the opportunity to meet people from other karate schools. It is often exciting and informative to watch practitioners of other karate styles display their skills. You can also have a chance to match your skill with students of equal rank from other schools.

If you think you would like to enter a tournament, discuss it with your instructor. He or she will tell you if you are ready to compete. It is important to remember that not everyone who studies karate enters such contests. Many people prefer to attend tournaments as spectators, not as competitors. This is perfectly fine; if you do not wish to compete you will not be required to do so.

If you are to compete in sparring, your opponent will be called to enter the ring from the side opposite you. The referee will have you bow to him and then to each other.

You will spar for two minutes or until one of you receives three points. After two minutes, whoever has scored the most points will win. If you both have an equal number of points (for example, two each) the match will go into another two-minute period called an "overtime." The first person to score a point during the overtime will win the match.

Some tournaments will allow very light contact to the body while others will not. It is important to know ahead of time whether the rules will allow such contact. Contact to the face is never permitted. Anyone who actually hits his opponent in the face is automatically disqualified. During sparring contests you will wear foam pads on your hands and feet. This is an added precaution against injury and the pads are worn even when the no-contact rule is in effect.

Tournaments also have kata competition. A kata is a prearranged sequence of blocks, punches and kicks, simulating actual combat with several attackers. For kata, there are usually five judges who will sit facing you. You should bow to them and then announce your name, the style you have studied, and the name of the kata you will do. Speak in a loud confident voice. Do not be timid when you speak.

Judges will watch to see if you maintain proper balance and correct form. You must do each move as if really confronting an opponent. Your blocks, strikes, and kicks should be strong and forceful. Of course, the judges will also expect you to remember all of the movements of your particular kata.

If you realize you have left out a movement, it is usually better just to continue with the kata. Above all, do not frown, shake your head or look displeased. If you forget what to do, you will be allowed one chance to start over again.

After you have finished, the five judges will indicate how many points he or she is giving you. Each judge will award you between one and ten points. The highest and the lowest scores will be dropped. The other three will be averaged to give you your final score. It is very rare to receive a score of nine or ten. A score of seven or above is considered to be quite good.

After you are told your score, you will bow to the judges and then leave the ring. Never argue or pout if you disagree with your score. The self-discipline of karate means that you accept the score and still express good manners to the officials.

A karate proverb states that in a match there is always a winner but never a loser. As long as a person has tried, he cannot be considered a loser. What is important is that the person has done his best, even if the other person has gotten more points. Effort and a willingness to try are what counts the most in karate.

It is important that you try your best, and that you enjoy what you are doing. Do not worry about surpassing others; think only of improving what you yourself can do. The progress you make should be seen in relationship to you. Do not compare yourself to others and do not get discouraged. No two people are exactly alike, and no two people will learn or perform karate exactly the same way. It is more important to enjoy what you are doing than to worry about how well you are doing.

10   Self-Defense

One day a karate master and three of his students were walking in the woods. They soon found that their path was blocked by a wild horse. The karate master asked the students what they would do to avoid being kicked by the horse.

"I would grab one of the horse's legs," said the first student. "Then the horse would be unable to kick me."

The second student replied, "I would run towards the horse and vault over his back to avoid being kicked."

"I," said the third student, "would take another path and go around the horse to avoid being kicked."

The karate master scolded the first student. "Your answer relies on strength. That is not the true way of karate. You still have much to learn."

To the second student he said, "You rely too much on speed. That is not the true way of karate, either. You, too, have much to learn."

Then the karate master smiled at the third student. "You truly understand karate!" he exclaimed. "You would go out of your way to avoid danger. You have learned your lessons very well."

This parable illustrates what self-defense should mean to a karate student. The best defense is to avoid trouble. Karate students are taught to walk away from challenges. They learn to ignore teasing and provocation from others.

There are times, however, when you cannot avoid trouble. Situations may arise in which you must use physical means to defend yourself because all other means have failed.

The following techniques show how to defend yourself from common types of attack. When practicing with a partner remember to work slowly. Make sure you do not really hit each other. Learn to rely on proper form rather than strength. Work cooperatively with each other and you will both learn how to defend yourselves.

Defense Against a Choke

The attacker grabs the defender around the neck and begins to choke her. She grabs his left arm with her right hand. Then she steps back

with her right foot while bringing her left arm across in front of her chest. She then swings her left elbow into her attacker's face.

Defense Against a Bear Hug

The boy on the right grabs the smaller boy under the arm, lifting him off the ground in a bear hug. The defender slaps his palms against the

attacker's ears. This will cause the attacker to release his hold. The boy on the left now grabs the attacker's hair. He pulls him downward while driving his knee into the attacker's midsection.

Defense Against a Hair Grab

The attacker applies a painful hair grab. The defender grabs the attacker's hand and presses it to her head. This will relieve the pain of the

hair pull. She then drives the palm of her hand upward under the attacker's chin. She then moves her hand to the attacker's shoulder and pushes him backward while sweeping his leg out from under him.

Defense Against a Wrist Grab

The attacker grabs the defender's wrist. The defender then pulls his hand towards his own body while, at the same time, doing a side kick to the attacker's midsection.

Defense Against a Headlock

The attacker grabs the defender in a headlock. The defender hits the back of the attacker's knee with her own knee. This will cause him to loosen his hold on her neck. She then reaches her arm up, over, and around the attacker's head. She then straightens up as she pushes his head back with her arm. She continues to push with her arm until the attacker falls over backwards.

11 The Endless Path

Where to Next?

If you have enjoyed this book, you may wish to learn more by enrolling in a karate class. You can look in the yellow pages of the phone book under "Karate Instruction" for a listing of the schools in your area. Sometimes community centers or the neighborhood YMCA–YWCA will also offer karate classes. You can call them to ask if they have a karate class or if they can refer you to one.

Visit some of the schools in your area. Invite your parents to accompany you. The particular type of karate being taught is not as important as the attitude of the instructor. Watch how he or she conducts the class. The karate class should be run the way any other class is run. The students should enjoy what they are learning. They should also be respectful of the teacher and each other.

Do not let the appearance of the karate school fool you. The karate lessons available in a fancy, carpeted, air-conditioned school are not necessarily any better than those offered in the basement of a community center. *What* you learn is more important than *where* you learn it.

Most karate schools charge on a monthly basis. Often there is a discount if you agree to take a specific number of lessons. It is usually better, however, to avoid paying for too many lessons in advance until you decide if you really like the class.

The Endless Path

Karate is a challenge. It will challenge you mentally and physically. And, if you accept the challenge, you will benefit mentally and physically. As you stick with it, you will find that progress brings new challenges and new benefits. If you accept the challenge you will begin to walk what is called the "Endless Path." You will never be bored as you walk the Endless Path because there will always be more to learn, more to do, and more to enjoy.

INDEX